All About
Frederick Douglass

D1511117

Robin L. Condon

BLUE RIVER PRESS

Indianapolis, Indiana

All About Frederick Douglass
Copyright © 2016 Robin L. Condon

Published by Blue River Press
Indianapolis, Indiana
www.brpressbooks.com

Distributed by Cardinal Publishers Group
Tom Doherty Company, Inc.
www.cardinalpub.com

All rights reserved under International and
Pan-American Copyright Conventions.

No part of this book may be reproduced, stored in a
database or other retrieval system, or transmitted in any
form, by any means, including mechanical, photocopy,
recording or otherwise, without the prior written
permission of the publisher.

ISBN: 978-1-68157-090-7

Author: Robin L. Condon
Series Editor: Charleen Davis
Editor: Dani McCormick
Interior Illustrator: Bryan Janky
Book Design: Dave Reed
Cover Artist: Jennifer Mujezinovic
Cover Design: David Miles

Printed in the United States of America

Contents

For my mother,
Antonia Newman Jaslow,
who taught hundreds of children,
including me.

Frederick Douglass as a young man

All About
Frederick Douglass

Preface

Frederick Douglass was one of the best-known African Americans of the nineteenth-century. He was born into slavery, but learned to read and write, and mastered public speaking. After his successful escape from slavery in September of 1838, he began reading abolitionist William Lloyd Garrison's newspaper, the *Liberator*. Garrison became so impressed by Douglass that he recruited him as a lecturer for his Massachusetts Anti-Slavery Society.

In addition to delivering thousands of lectures on the antislavery circuit in the northeastern United States, he wrote his autobiography three separate times, edited and published three newspapers, and wrote numerous editorials and essays, some poetry, and a novella. In his later life, Douglass was appointed to several government positions. He corresponded with famous figures and his books, especially his first autobiography, *Narrative of the Life of Frederick Douglass, An American Slave* (1845), became well-known all over the world and were published in many languages during Douglass's lifetime. It continues to be taught in middle-school, high school, and college nearly two centuries after its publication.

Abraham
Lincoln
(1861-1865)

Andrew
Johnson
(1865-1869)

Ulysses
S. Grant
(1869-1877)

Rutherford
B. Hayes
(1877-1881)

Douglass advised the eight American presidents from Abraham Lincoln to Benjamin Harrison. He also recruited African Americans to fight in the Civil War and worked for their equality. Not only did Frederick Douglass advance the cause of abolition of slavery in America, but he also worked to promote the rights of all oppressed groups, especially women. Douglass envisioned a country that, after the bloody Civil War, would provide equal standing in the law for all Americans of different races and genders, whether they be immigrants or native born citizens.

Douglass's hopes for universal justice were not realized during his lifetime. Yet, his work advanced those goals a great deal. Douglass's efforts had a great impact on the events of the 19th, 20th, and 21st centuries in America. He influenced African

James A.
Garfield
(1881-1881)

Chester A.
Arthur
(1881-1885)

Grover
Cleveland
(1885-1889)

Benjamin
Harrison
(1889-1893)

American activists, educators, intellectuals, and political leaders whose own work benefited from the great orator's legacy. Among those were Booker T. Washington, Ida B. Wells, and W. E. B. Du Bois.

His life and death were subjects for poet Paul Laurence Dunbar. Douglass's powerful words laid the foundation for the work of the Reverend Dr. Martin Luther King, Jr., and others. The first African American President of the United States, Barack Obama, frequently utilized Douglass's political speeches in the classes he taught at the

University of Chicago Law School. Douglass's life remains a source of inspiration to Americans, and people throughout the world.

Middle-aged Frederick Douglass

Chapter One
<u>Growing Up</u>

The boy who would one day name himself "Frederick Douglass" was born in Tuckahoe on the Eastern Shore of Maryland in February 1818.

His mother, Harriet Bailey, was born a slave in 1792. Frederick would never learn the name of his father, but since his skin was much lighter than his mother's, he presumed his father was a white man. The name Harriet gave baby Frederick at birth was Frederick Augustus Washington Bailey. Harriet was hired out to work on another farm miles away, so Frederick was raised by his grandparents. Betsey Bailey had been born a slave sometime around the year 1775. Isaac Bailey was a sawyer, or woodchopper, in trade.

The Bailey family, which consisted of Frederick's grandparents, his aunts, uncles, and young cousins under the age of six, lived in a wooden cabin with a clay floor next to Tuckahoe Creek. In slave families, elderly relatives would often care for the smallest children in the family while their mothers and fathers labored in the fields or in the homes of their owners.

Among Eastern Shore slaves, the Bailey family was an old and a proud one. The family came to America not from Africa directly, but from Barbados, part of the British-held West Indies. Among American slaves, the Bailey family was considered elite.

Frederick's grandmother, in particular, was well-respected among the Tuckahoe slaves not only for her family connections, but because she was highly skilled in growing vegetables and catching fish. Grandmother Betsey was a capable midwife and helped the sick too.

Frederick and his cousins were happy in their grandparents' house. Still, sometimes the adults would talk about someone they called "Old Master" in hushed voices. They did not want the little ones to hear about the hard lives that they would eventually lead.

One morning, Grandmother Betsey took Frederick on a long walk of nearly twelve miles. He was about six or seven-years-old, and struggled to keep up with his grandmother. By the end of that hot afternoon, they had reached "Old Master's" house on the Lloyd Plantation.

Frederick noticed the terribly sad look on Grandmother's face. She introduced him to an older boy whom she said was his brother Perry and to some girls she told him were his big sisters Sarah and Eliza. Frederick had heard his family speak of Perry, Sarah, and Eliza, but he did not know that they were his brother and sisters. He had never seen them!

Great House Farm (Edward Lloyd's Wye House), where Aaron Anthony's (Douglass' first master) house was located

After some time, his grandmother went away, very quietly. When Perry told him that she had gone, Frederick began to sob as though he would never stop, feeling abandoned in an unfamiliar world, even though many children, including his brother and sisters, surrounded him. He was now to live a very different life at "Old Master's" home.

Frederick walked to his new home with his Grandmother Betsey in about 1824

"Old Master's" name was Captain Aaron Anthony. He owned several farms in Tucka-hoe, and he worked as chief clerk and butler to

Colonel Edward Lloyd, who owned one of the largest plantations in the state of Maryland. Captain Anthony's house was located on the Lloyd plantation, and his cook, Aunt Katy, also a slave and relative of the Bailey family, cared for the slave children Anthony owned. Aunt Katy was not kind or motherly except to her own children. They were given more food and better clothing. Frederick often had to go to bed without eating, and with only a burlap sack as covering.

One night, he was so hungry that he had tried to roast some grains of corn he found in the cooking fire embers. A young woman startled him, scooping the grains from his hand, and replacing them with a delicious ginger cake. She scolded Aunt Katy for mistreating the child, and lifted Frederick to her knee and held him while he ate.

The woman was Harriet, Frederick's mother; he had only seen her four or five times in his life because she worked on a different farm. She had traveled more than twelve hard miles on foot that evening to see her young son and would have to travel back before sunrise. Frederick fell asleep in her arms. But by morning she was gone.

Frederick's bed was uncomfortable with only a burlap sack on the hard floor

Frederick never saw his mother again, and he heard of her death a short time later. He did learn two important facts: that she loved him, and that it was rumored in Tuckahoe that she knew how to read. Frederick's vague memory of his mother's kindness to him and his belief in her literacy instilled in him the desire for knowledge at a very early age.

Despite Aunt Katy's tyranny, Frederick managed somehow to become acquainted with Daniel Lloyd, the youngest son of the wealthy family who employed Aaron Anthony. The choice of Frederick as the companion of Daniel Lloyd was one of the first instances of Frederick's amazing luck. We do not know the reason Frederick was chosen for this comparatively easy and fun duty.

Daniel was five years Frederick's senior, and Frederick was both servant and friend to the wealthy young man. Among the benefits, occasionally, was extra food. It may have been from Daniel, too, that Frederick learned to speak standard, rather than plantation, English.

Frederick was a favorite, too, of Anthony's daughter Lucretia, newly-married to Thomas Auld, a ship captain and employee of Aaron Anthony. The clever, charming, and attractive boy determined that he could earn bread and butter by singing outside Lucretia's window and he did so often.

"Mrs. Lucretia," might have been responsible for choosing Frederick to work in the Baltimore home of her brother-in-law, Hugh Auld. There Frederick would serve as a guardian and companion to Hugh and Sophia Auld's son,

Tommy. Lucretia provided Frederick with new clothes. She gave the boy his first treasured pair of trousers for life in the city.

Mrs. Lucretia gave Frederick his first pair of trousers as a going away present when he moved to the city

So, while still a young child, Frederick was removed from the life of a typical plantation slave. His two years on the Lloyd plantation afforded him brutal stories to tell. Most of these were secondhand, told in the slave quarters, though he did witness some beatings.

Even though he was leaving all the people he knew on the Eastern Shore of Maryland, Frederick was not sad. He had seen and heard enough on the Lloyd plantation, to realize what his future there would hold. He was ready for something new.

Chapter 2
His First Sojourn in Baltimore

For days before the scheduled journey on the Lloyd's sloop, a small sail boat named the *Sally Lloyd*, Frederick worried that his trip would be canceled. But, on what was probably March 18, 1826, he boarded the sloop, sporting his new trousers.

Frederick experienced, for the first time, the view of the famous dome of the capitol building in Annapolis, Maryland. He reached his destination and was delivered to the home of Hugh and Sophia Auld in Baltimore's shipping district, Fells Point. Baltimore proved a great shock to the country boy who, at about eight years old, had never seen dwellings by the row or such well-dressed people strolling in the streets. Perhaps the biggest surprise was that most of the people, African Americans included, wore shoes.

The Hugh Auld family was not wealthy, and they were unaccustomed to slaveholding. Mrs.

Auld, in particular, was grateful for the help Frederick would provide for her in caring for her two-year-old son, Tommy; she did not consider his work her right, but rather a luxury. She viewed him more as a new member of the household than as a slave to be used or abused according to her whims.

Aliceanna Street in Fells Point was part of the shipping district, putting Hugh Auld close to work

Perhaps because the Fells Point Aulds had not experienced directly the way slaves were treated in the agricultural regions of the Maryland, they provided Frederick with comforts that plantation slaves seldom enjoyed. He had his own loft room above the kitchen—a room that contained a real bed with a quilt and blankets. That night, Frederick ate a proper supper at a table and went to bed with a full stomach.

Frederick spent his days in the company of Sophia Auld and little Tommy, and for the first time since leaving his grandmother's cabin, he felt like part of an affectionate family. Sophia was warm and motherly, and Tommy was an agreeable and pleasant child.

Hugh Auld was not nearly as welcoming to Frederick as were his wife and son. Working at the time as a ship's carpenter, he spent most of the day in the shipyard and often returned home in the evening drunk and irritable. Even so, Frederick's life in Fells Point was a vast improvement.

Sophia Auld, although raised on the Eastern Shore, was never a part of the wealthy slaveholding class. Her parents were devout Methodists who believed that slavery was a crime against God, man, and nature. Before her marriage, she had worked as a weaver. Because of her working-class background and her religious devotion, it is not surprising that she treated Frederick as she would any intelligent and charming child, regardless of his skin color and status.

Frederick's happiness in the Auld home was short-lived. Captain Anthony, "Old Master," was still his legal owner. Anthony died in November of 1826, leaving no will and no evidence that he intended to gift Frederick to the Fells Point Auld family. Frederick was returned to the Eastern Shore in October of 1827, in order to be given, along with Anthony's other properties, to his heirs.

He would soon learn that his beloved Mrs. Lucretia had died and that her widower, Thomas Auld, would inherit her portion of the estate. Again, the young slave was remarkably lucky in two ways; first, he was given to Thomas Auld, rather than to Aaron Anthony's harsh son Andrew. Second, and more importantly, Thomas Auld returned him to the family of his brother Hugh Auld in Baltimore in November of 1827.

Hugh Auld started his own shipping business in 1827, where he built ships alongside his workers

By that time, Hugh Auld had started his own shipbuilding business, and had moved his family to a rented house on Philpot Street, on the north side of the Fells Point hook. In his new neighborhood, Frederick met many boys his own age, most of whom were the white sons of master carpenters and ship fitters. His close friendships taught him that skin color prejudice was not a natural human emotion—he did not find it in his young white friends, who treated him as an equal.

Inside the Auld's new home—Frederick began to listen closely to Sophia as she read her Bible aloud. To him, the transformation from printed letters to meaningful language was a magical process, and Sophia's reading motivated Frederick to ask her to teach him to read. She readily complied, and very quickly Frederick learned the alphabet and was able to recognize short words.

Sophia Auld helped Frederick further his education by reading the Bible to him and motivating him

Sophia, proud of his intelligence and accomplishment, informed her husband of her activities. She did not expect that her husband would angrily demand that she stop teaching the child at once. Knowledge would make a slave unhappy with his lot, he told his wife. Once a slave had acquired some knowledge, he would desire more and would ultimately either escape from slavery or become useless in that role.

Frederick would later recall Hugh Auld's warning to his wife as the first antislavery lecture he ever heard. From that moment on, he resolved to become literate and to acquire as much knowledge as possible. His Baltimore master had revealed to him the key to gaining his freedom: he must learn to read and write.

Chapter Three
Reading and Writing

Hugh Auld's warning to his wife Sophia frightened her, and her attitude toward Frederick changed to that of a stern mistress. He would later write that, when he had books or newspapers Mrs. Sophia "would rush at me with the utmost fury, snatch the book or paper from my hand, with something of the wrath and consternation which a traitor might be disposed to feel on being discovered in a plot by some dangerous spy."

It was painful for him to see the good woman torn between her husband's rules and her own conscience. Even though her anger was directed at him, he felt sympathy for her.

He understood that he must make other plans to learn. He settled on the idea of using his friends, the white boys he had met on the street, as his teachers. Frederick always carried a copy of Webster's *Spelling Book* in his pocket so that in his free time or on his errands he might have a lesson in spelling. His friends encouraged Frederick to hope for freedom, telling him that "they did not believe God ever made anyone to be a slave."

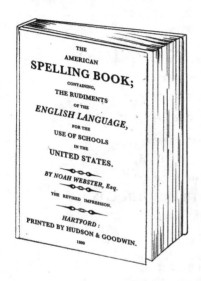

When he was thirteen years old, Frederick discovered another book that would remain important to him. Having earned some pocket money on the street by shining shoes, he purchased *The Columbian Orator*. This very popular children's schoolbook was a collection of famous speeches, and it contained instructions for making speeches. His friends were memorizing passages from the book to recite at school, and Frederick eagerly joined in.

One particularly meaningful piece in the book for him was a short dialogue between a master and his slave. The slave successfully defends him-self from all of his master's claims to ownership. At the end, the master frees his slave and wishes him well. Studying *The Columbian Orator* provided Frederick with the words to voice his thoughts.

THE

COLUMBIAN ORATOR:

CONTAINING

A VARIETY OF

Original and Selected PIECES:

TOGETHER WITH

R U L E S;

CALCULATED

TO IMPROVE YOUTH AND OTHERS IN THE

ORNAMENTAL AND USEFUL

ART OF ELOQUENCE

By CALEB BINGHAM, *A.M.*

Author of the American Preceptor, Young Lady's Accidence, &

"CATO-cultivated ELOQUENCE, as a necessary mean for de-defending THE RIGHTS OF THE PEOPLE, and for enforcing good Counsels."   ROLLIN.

FIFTEENTH EDITION.

Bofton:

Printed by MANNING & LORIN ,

For the AUTHOR: and fold at his Book-Store, No.44

CORNHILL, and by the BOOKSELLERS in general.

April, 1812.

The *Columbian Orator* was a common school book of the time and provided Frederick with words to describe his ideas

Speeches about the American Revolution and other arguments for liberty and justice moved him deeply. Frederick wrote, "The reading of these speeches added much to my limited stock of knowledge, and enabled me to give tongue to many interesting thoughts which had often flashed through my mind and died away for want of words to give them utterance." As his knowledge grew, however, so did his misery in the state of slavery.

Frederick grew more determined to gain the skills that would help him become free. He encountered the words: "abolition" and "abolitionists." Knowing that people were working and praying for the end of slavery gave Frederick hope. He was not alone in his struggle.

Frederick believed that God was on the side of the abolitionists and that He had sent cholera to Baltimore as a punishment for slavery. Frederick found support for these beliefs in African American preacher "Father" Charles Lawson, who encouraged him to pray and to learn the Bible. Father Lawson told him that the

"Lord had a great work for [him] to do" and that "[He] must prepare to do it."

Frederick knew that learning to read and write was the key to his freedom

Frederick knew that one day he would attempt to escape from slavery. In preparation, he must learn to write. At the time, the only way slaves could travel without their masters was to carry a pass, signed by the master, permitting them to go to a set place at a given time or date. Frederick decided that the best way to escape was to forge a pass and travel to a free state where he could find abolitionists who would help him.

Before he could carry out his plan, however, he needed to learn to write. Frederick started copying the letters that marked the timber in the shipyards. When Frederick mastered each letter, he would challenge his friends to form the letter. In this way, he perfected his own writing of the letters he knew, but they taught him new ones too.

Frederick moved a flour barrel into his loft bedroom to use as a desk. To practice writing, he would rewrite the Tommy Auld's used school copy-books. He would also copy pages from the Bible and Methodist hymnal. As he tried to improve his handwriting, though, a new obstacle threatened to disrupt his plans.

Chapter Four
<u>Return to the Eastern Shore</u>

A quarrel between brothers Thomas and Hugh Auld over the fate of Frederick's cousin Henny caused Thomas to call Frederick back to St. Michaels, Maryland. Henny was the daughter of Frederick's Aunt Milly. Henny had fallen into a fire when she was a baby, and the burns caused her to lose the use of her hands. Henny could never be useful as a slave, but was kept in the Auld home while kind Mrs. Lucretia was alive. Thomas and his second wife Rowena did not want to waste resources on Henny. They sent her to Baltimore to work in Hugh's household. But the Baltimore household could not make use of her.

Unlike Mrs. Lucretia, the Hugh Auld family had no sentimental attachment to Henny, and they sent her back to Thomas. Thomas, angry at Hugh's ingratitude, decided that if his brother refused to keep Henny, he could not keep

Frederick either. In 1833, sixteen year old Frederick had to leave his friends in Baltimore. He would miss Father Lawson and all of the boys whose companionship had been so important to him.

Frederick had become a young man, and after years of life in the city, he was unaccustomed to the hardships of slave life that he would find

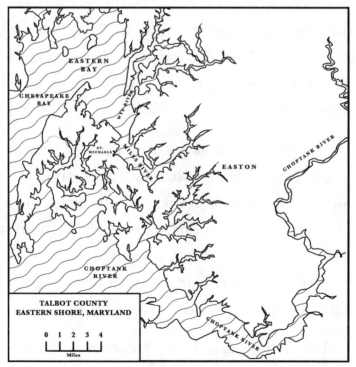

Talbot County, Maryland, was full of harbors and ports where a shipbuilder could make a living

at Thomas Auld's home. He was outraged that Rowena Auld kept food under lock and key. He reasoned that, as the property of Thomas, he had been deprived of the benefits of his own labor, so he began to steal food.

By August of 1833, Frederick had become deeply miserable and difficult for his master to manage. He was angry and strong, and thought often about his escape. When Thomas Auld was converted to Methodism at a Camp Meeting that month, Frederick began to hope that this would lead to improved circumstances for his slaves.

Frederick found some relief in attending and teaching at a local Sabbath-school with African American adults and children. But that ended when his master, along with other Methodist leaders, mobbed and destroyed the little Sabbath-school, threatening to shoot anyone who dared to organize such meetings again.

The most tragic thing Frederick witnessed, however, was Thomas' brutal beating of Cousin Henny. The St. Michaels Aulds had been trying to rid themselves of the responsibility of caring for Henny, but they were unable to give her to relatives without finding her returned almost immediately. Thomas vented his frustration by flogging the girl mercilessly. Finally, Henny was left to starve, as she was physically incapable of providing for herself.

Thomas Auld did not respond well to Frederick's repeated disobedience

Frederick despaired; he had begun to escape to a neighboring farm where he could get a meal from the cook on a regular basis. After nine months and several beatings, Thomas decided that he could not endure Frederick's behavior any longer. He sent him away, "to be broken."

Frederick was hired out to tenant farmer Edward Covey, a noted slave breaker in the area. Covey had the labor of the slaves nearly free of charge, and in turn, legal masters would have their slaves trained by the cruel and relentless Covey. Following a particularly savage beating, Frederick sought the help of Thomas Auld, running back to St. Michaels to show his master what had been done to his property. Auld was angry at Covey for damaging one of his most valuable slaves, but was also angry with Frederick for creating more trouble.

Because Auld did not want to lose the wages of Frederick's labor by allowing him to leave Covey's farm before his one-year contract had expired, Frederick was sent back to endure the remainder of his training. His master's indifference to his abuse had changed Frederick. He now resolved that if Covey tried to beat him again, he would do everything he could to defend himself.

He did not have to wait long. Covey left him alone on the Sunday he returned, but the next morning, as Frederick was caring for the horses, Covey snuck into the stable in an attempt to tie up and beat the wayward slave. This time, Frederick was ready to fight back.

Slave cabins were bare and cold, with little furniture and no comforts to make them feel like home

Covey, frightened by Frederick's power, called upon the other slaves on his farm to help him. But they did not come to his aid, even though they knew they would be beaten for ignoring his pleas. After two hours of fighting, he let go of

Frederick, telling him to go back to work.

Covey never tried to beat him again and Frederick gained a reputation among local slaves and masters as being a slave who was hard to whip. Rumors of his literacy spread too, and local slaveholders feared him as a bad influence on other slaves.

In January of 1835, Frederick began work at the farm of William Freeland, three miles from St. Michaels. Freeland, unlike Covey or even Thomas Auld, was "a Southern gentleman" with grand notions of honor. He treated his slaves fairly and honestly by the standards of the time. He did not overwork them, and he fed them enough to keep them in good health.

On Freeland's farm, Frederick found friends among his fellow slaves and returned to his books. He established a small outdoor Sabbath-school where at times he had more than forty students learning to read and write under his instruction. The need to survive that had overtaken him during the harsh year with Covey was replaced with his old yearning for liberty.

A year passed without misery, but also without happiness. Freeland renewed his contract for Frederick's labor for the next year, 1836. Frederick surveyed his past and planned for his future. His most important plan for the new year was to escape from slavery into freedom!

Frederick was relieved to live in peace and relative comfort at the Freeland farm, but he was far from content. He was able to form friendships with other young slaves in his neighborhood and recruited five to join him in his escape to a free state. The group of hopeful slaves met on Sunday evenings in the early months of 1836 in order to plan.

Frederick inspired the other slaves to escape
with him on Easter of 1836

Sometimes they were optimistic and excited by the prospect of freedom. Other times they were afraid, imagining the many obstacles they would encounter. They knew that they could be captured and punished, even killed, by their own masters. They also could be kidnapped by slave traders and sold into situations far worse than their current one.

The plan was to take a large canoe owned by Mr. Hambleton (Thomas Auld's father-in-law) the night before Easter and paddle seventy miles to the northernmost part of Chesapeake Bay. Reaching land, they would set the canoe adrift and travel on foot, guided by the North Star, to a free state.

The group thought their chances of success were greater if they traveled part of the way by water—if anyone saw them they could be mistaken for fishermen in service of their master. Traveling by land was more treacherous because any white man had the right to stop them and demand their free papers.

But in spite of their very real fears, the six young men pursued their plan. Frederick wrote passes for himself and each member of his company.

> *"This is to certify that I, the undersigned, have given the bearer, my servant John, full liberty to go to Baltimore to spend the Easter holidays.*
>
> *W. H.*
> *"Near St. Michaels, Talbot Co., Md."*

Frederick and his friends all carried similar travel passes during their escape attempt

The group did not plan to show these passes to anyone, except as a last resort. They understood the importance of appearing calm and composed during the escape. They even rehearsed how they would behave if they were questioned. Still they were anxious.

The young men waited for the day of their escape. That morning, Fredrick was seized by the vivid thought that the plan had been betrayed! Frederick soon saw that he had been right: three constables along with Mr. Freeland and Mr. Hambleton approached.

They grabbed Frederick, restraining him along with his friend John Harris. Then Henry Harris was called out of the barn and told to cross his hands so that the constables could tie him as well. Henry refused, and fought with them. During the scuffle, Frederick was able to throw his fake travel pass into the fire without anyone noticing.

The travel passes could get them in trouble, so Frederick quickly burned them in the nearby fire

Henry was overpowered and restrained with his two friends. The two masters and the constables began to search for the passes they had heard Frederick had written. Then Mr. Freeland's mother came from the kitchen with biscuits for John and Henry's breakfast, screaming at Frederick that everything was his fault, and that her slaves John and Henry Harris, who had grown up in her house, would never dream of leaving her.

The group of young men were tied to the horses and dragged toward Easton to be imprisoned. They were tied close enough that they could speak together on the journey. They decided to admit nothing of the plan.

At Easton, they faced the torment of slave traders and agents, who swarmed the jail to size them up and plan where they would be sold. The slave traders threatened Frederick and his friends. But after Easter ended, the young Harris men were released into the custody of their masters. For a week he was alone, and he imagined all sorts of terrifying scenes his future might hold. Finally, Thomas Auld appeared at the prison to claim him.

Chapter Five
Apprenticeship in Baltimore and Escape

Thomas Auld's father-in-law, William Hambleton, considered Frederick a dangerous influence on other slaves. He warned Auld that he would shoot Frederick if he stayed on the Eastern Shore.

Rather than lose a young, strong, and valuable slave, Auld had planned a safe and profitable alternative: Frederick would learn a trade that would generate income for his master's family. If he behaved, his master told him, he would be freed at the age of twenty-five.

Again Frederick dared to hope. He was going back to Hugh Auld's household in Baltimore, and it was possible that in seven years he might be a free man. For his part, Frederick was delighted to return to the place he missed.

Unfortunately, the Auld household had changed. Little Tommy had grown up, and no longer treated Frederick with affection, but with the contempt he had learned to feel towards slaves. Frederick had loved and cared for Tommy; he was hurt by the boy's new attitude. But he was not in Baltimore to care for Tommy, he was there to work in the shipyards of Fells Point. He learned to be a caulker, which meant he filled cracks in boat planks. Master Hugh had gotten Frederick a job at William Gardner's shipyard, where two large man-of-war vessels were being built for the Mexican government.

Frederick worked on all types of boats from small schooners (left) to larger clippers (right)

Over one hundred men, mostly carpenters, worked in the shipyard. They had no time to teach Frederick, so they used him as a servant. It was hard for Frederick to keep up with the demands of four or five different chores at once. The carpenters would threaten Frederick with beatings if he failed to meet their expectations quickly.

When he had been at Gardner's Shipyard for eight months, Frederick was attacked by white carpenters and laborers who beat him savagely, almost knocking one of his eyes out of its socket. Hiring slaves benefited the shipyard owners financially, but it threatened the livelihoods of the poor bitterly resentful whites because slaves were cheaper workers.

When Hugh Auld saw Frederick's condition after the brutal beating, he was very angry. He brought Frederick to the judge, but because the testimony of the white laborers was given credit, and no African American witnesses could testify, Auld was unable to get justice for himself and his slave. He withdrew Frederick from

Gardner's Shipyard and brought him to Walter Price's Yard, where Auld served as foreman.

Frederick became an expert caulker, a skill
his master benefited from through his wages

There, Frederick quickly learned to use his caulker's tools. After a year, he had become an expert caulker who could earn the highest wages paid to journeymen caulkers in Baltimore. Other caulkers befriended him, and the free blacks among them invited him to join their educational organization, the East Baltimore Mental Improvement Society.

Frederick often took part in the Society's debates and proved himself to be a skillful and eloquent debater. This made him revisit the justice of slavery and his place in it. "Why is Hugh Auld entitled to the wages from my labor?" he asked himself, forming reasoned arguments proving that a person's wages should be his own. That is when Frederick began to plot his next attempt at escape.

While attending gatherings of the East Baltimore Mental Improvement Society, he met Anna Murray, the daughter of two former slaves who had purchased their own freedom. Anna was her parents' first child to be born into freedom. She worked as a housemaid to earn a living. Frederick and Anna fell in love and planned to marry. Anna would help him to escape, and once he reached a free state, he would send for her. After she joined him, they would marry.

In order to put his plans in motion, he needed Master Hugh Auld to watch him less closely. If he could persuade Thomas Auld, his legal owner, to allow him to hire out his own time, he might have greater freedom to plan his escape.

Anna Murray Douglass would become a leader of the Boston Female Anti-Slavery Society after her marriage to Douglass

After some thought, Master Hugh agreed to allow Frederick this freedom on certain conditions: Frederick would have to find his own jobs, he would have to pay for his lodging, food, clothing, and work tools with his wages, and he would give what remained to his master. Frederick convinced Hugh that it would be more profitable for him to allow Frederick to make his own arrangements.

Accumulating money by hiring his own labor proved difficult for Frederick at first. He had to work long hours to pay Master Hugh and support himself. But with hard work and thrift, he was able to save small amounts of money each week. The money would help him finance his escape. The date of his departure was set for Monday, September 3, 1838.

In his last escape attempt, Frederick had forged travel passes in order to travel without a master. But there was another way a slave could travel without his master. African American men were allowed to be sailors, and as sailors, would hold "sailors' papers". These papers contained detailed descriptions of the men who held them, and at the top of the pass was an etching of an American eagle, which gave the document authority.

Frederick was able to borrow the sailors' papers from a friend who bore only a slight resemblance to him. His friend was quite a bit darker than Frederick. He could only hope that authorities would not check the papers carefully.

Frederick had a plan to avoid the railroad officials. His friend, Isaac Rolls, a hackman, which was a hired carriage driver, brought his luggage to the train as it was departing, and Frederick jumped onto the train as it was in motion. He was dressed as a sailor, and it is believed that Anna sewed the uniform for him.

Even though Frederick looked like a sailor and was traveling in the car reserved for African

GOLDEN DEARTH, PRINTER, WARREN, R.I.

UNITED STATES 🦅 **OF AMERICA.**

DISTRICT AND PORT OF BRISTOL.
STATE OF RHODE ISLAND AND PROVIDENCE PLANTATIONS.

I CHARLES COLLINS, Collector of the District aforesaid, do hereby that *Joseph Gladoling* an American seaman, aged *twenty one* years, or thereabouts, of the height of *five* feet *eight* inches, *fresh complexion, dark hair, blue eyes, a mole on his right cheek, one on his left arm* has produced to me proof in the manner directed in the Act of the United States of America, entitled *"An Act for the relief and protection of American Seamen,"* and pursuant to the said Act, I do hereby certify, that the said *Joseph Gladoling* is a citizen of the United States of America.

IN WITNESS WHEREOF, I have hereunto set my hand and seal of office, this *sixth* day of *February* one thousand eight hundred and *twelve*

Frederick used his friend's sailor's papers to escape on a train and ride north

Americans, a conductor approached him and demanded his free papers. Frederick had a ready answer: "I never carry my free papers to sea with me," he said. He took his sailor's protection out of his pocket, saying, "I have a paper with an American eagle on it, and that will carry me around the world."

Luckily the conductor did not look closely at the paper, and he left Frederick alone. But Frederick was still frightened because he saw several people on the train who would have recognized him if he had not been dressed as a sailor. He left the train in Philadelphia, asking an African American man how to get to New York. The man directed him, and Frederick embarked for New York. The journey from slavery to freedom took him less than twenty-four hours. He reached New York City that night.

He was now a fugitive from slavery. Even though he had his freedom, he had no friends and nowhere to go. He was free of slavery, but also free of food, shelter, and clothing. He did not know what to do, or whom to trust. If he asked another African American for advice, he risked betrayal. Sometimes free African Americans would alert kidnappers to the presence of a fugitive slave to receive a reward.

Finally, he saw a man that he had known well in slavery—a man known in Baltimore as "Allender's Jake" because he was owned by a Doctor Allender. Jake warned Frederick against asking anyone for help or seeking work at shipyards,

David Ruggles lived on Lispenard Street and helped many former slaves avoid recapture

because that would be one of the first places his master would look. Finally though, Frederick gathered his courage and approached a sailor. He asked for help.

Frederick was lucky; the sailor was a good man, and took him in for the night. In the morning he brought Frederick to Mr. David Ruggles, the secretary of the New York Vigilance Committee. This group, comprised of free blacks and antislavery whites, worked to clothe, feed, and shelter fugitive slaves.

Ruggles wrote for antislavery publications and delivered antislavery lectures. He introduced Frederick to other abolitionists, African American and white, who protected him from recapture.

Soon he was able to write to Anna so that she could join him in New York. The couple reunited and were married by Reverend J. W. C. Pennington, a well-known African American Presbyterian minister, who had himself escaped from slavery at the age of twenty-one. Since Frederick's trade was caulking, Ruggles suggested that the newlyweds head for New Bedford, Massachusetts, where there were many shipyards and caulking work was available.

Reverend J. W. C. Pennington married
the young couple in 1838

Anna and her husband took a steamer to Newport, Rhode Island; from there they attempted to reach New Bedford by a horse-drawn vehicle called a stagecoach. Unfortunately, the couple did not have enough money to pay the fare. Fortunately, two kind Quaker gentlemen offered to share the ride and pay the expenses.

Nathan Johnson, a conductor, or leader, on the Underground Railroad, met Frederick and

Anna, and paid what remained of their fare. The two stayed with the elderly Mr. and Mrs. Johnson for two weeks. Johnson suggested Frederick change his name from Frederick Bailey so he would be more difficult to find and return to slavery.

Johnson had been reading Walter Scott's poem "Lady of the Lake," and he suggested "Douglas," based on a heroic character in the tale. This name Frederick assumed, adding an "s" to the end of the name, as was the fashion at the time. This is how the slave Frederick Bailey became the free man Frederick Douglass.

Chapter Six
Douglass Becomes an Abolitionist Lecturer, Writer and Traveler

At first, everything seemed better in New Bedford. In the South, families that owned no slaves were considered "poor white trash," but, in New Bedford, wealthy families did not own slaves. African American families in Massachusetts owned more books than wealthy whites in Maryland. Johnson told Frederick that nothing in the Massachusetts Constitution would prevent an African American from becoming state governor, if he could be elected to the post. Black children attended the same public schools as white children.

Even at the shipyards, there were significant differences. The work done by twenty to thirty men in Baltimore was done with six men and an ox, allowing the businesses to gain more profit by paying fewer men. Douglass was shocked to see the conveniences in even the most modest homes: sinks, self-shutting drains, washing machines, wringing machines to help dry the washing and much more.

But in spite of all the advantages in Massachusetts, Douglass found securing a job as a caulker almost impossible because of race prejudice. White caulkers threatened to quit their jobs rather than accept an African American working beside them and earning the same wage. Douglass was forced to work for less pay and as a common laborer rather than as a trained caulker.

In order to support his wife, Douglass found that he had to take odd jobs to make up for the money he could not earn at the shipyard. Fortunately, he met with Mr. Joseph Ricketson, one of the Quakers who had shared the stagecoach ride with Frederick and Anna from the Newport Wharf. Mr. Ricketson owned an oil refinery and gave Douglass a job there.

After his stint at the oil refinery, he found work at George Howland's shipyard. His next job was at a brass factory. There, too, the foreman, Mr. Cobb, protected him from any abuse from his fellow workers.

One day, a young man approached Douglass, asking him to subscribe to an abolitionist newspaper, the *Liberator*, edited by the famous William Lloyd Garrison. Douglass had no money to subscribe, and told the solicitor that he had just recently escaped from slavery. The young man was moved by Douglass's story, and offered him a free subscription.

The Liberator, an abolitionist newspaper, gave Douglass a free subscription and influenced the way he thought about ending slavery

Reading the *Liberator* was a revelation to Douglass. The paper demanded the complete and immediate emancipation of all American slaves.

Douglass wrote that for him the *Liberator* was second in importance only to the Bible. Soon after, he began reading the newspaper regularly, he attended a lecture by Garrison and was deeply moved by his words of freedom. After this first lecture, Douglass attended all Garrison's speeches in New Bedford and took his first holiday from work in 1841 to attend a large antislavery convention in Nantucket.

William Lloyd Garrison founded the *Liberator* and firmly believed in ending slavery

John A. Collins, the general agent of the Massachusetts Anti-Slavery Society, who had heard Douglass speak at the small church where he and Anna worshipped in New Bedford approached Douglass. Collins asked him if he might speak about his experience in slavery before the Anti-Slavery Society. Douglass was nervous speaking before such a large audience comprised mostly of white people. But soon he had mesmerized the audience with tales of his experiences in slavery.

After the speech, Collins offered Douglass a job as an agent of the Society. Douglass would travel through Massachusetts and publicly advocate the Society's antislavery principles, using his own experiences to convince audiences of the wickedness of slavery. He would also secure new subscribers to the *Liberator* and the *Anti-Slavery Standard*, another abolitionist newspaper. Douglass believed that the fact that he had changed his name and did not reveal his master's name or his birthplace would keep him safe from being returned to slavery.

Frederick wanted to talk about the philosophy behind slavery and the reasons why it was wrong. However, the members of the Massachusetts Anti-Slavery Society believed that true stories of the violence and humiliation in slavery were what their audiences wanted to hear. His fellow abolitionists even urged Douglass to use plantation English in his speeches. They thought people would not believe he had ever been a slave because his diction, thanks to his study of *The Columbian Orator*, was so perfect.

They soon were proved correct. Audiences became skeptical about Douglass's origin and doubted whether someone so eloquent could have ever been a slave. After four years, the Massachusetts Anti-Slavery Society decided that the time had come for the fugitive slave to prove his true identity.

Garrison and his fellow abolitionist Wendell Phillips knew that it would be too dangerous for Frederick to reveal his identity in a public speech and decided that he must *write* the story of his life. He would reveal in print his name, Frederick

Bailey, and the names of his masters, as well as the locations where he was in enslaved. Frederick was only twenty-six when he began his autobiography, *Narrative of the Life of Frederick Douglass, An American Slave*. When the book was published in 1845, Garrison and Phillips feared for Douglass's safety. Douglass shared their fears, and he agreed to sail to England where he could not be captured by his former masters.

Wendell Phillips encouraged Frederick write his first autobiography and encouraged him to go to England for safety

Although he sailed on the "Cambria," a ship belonging to the British Cunard line, he experienced American color prejudice. He was not allowed a cabin in first class, but was forced into steerage. When he was invited by the ship's captain to give an antislavery lecture, passengers from Georgia and New Orleans threatened to throw him overboard.

After the ship arrived in England, Wendell Phillips acted as Douglass's guide; introducing him to distinguished and educated Englishmen and taking Douglass to hear parliamentary debates. Douglass was very popular in Ireland too, where he met the most famous advocate of ending the union between England and Ireland, Daniel O'Connell. He met literary stars as well, including author Hans Christian Andersen.

An edition of his *Narrative* was published in England and it sold very well. Douglass traveled throughout the British Isles delivering antislavery speeches to admiring audiences. He was able to enjoy public entertainments he would have been excluded from in the United States and was treated as an important celebrity. Douglass was amazed at how differently he was treated in other countries.

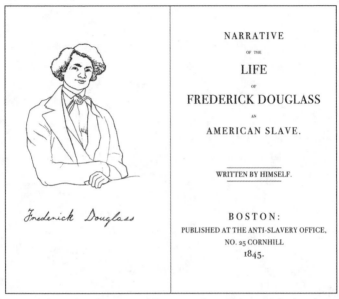

NARRATIVE

OF THE

LIFE

OF

FREDERICK DOUGLASS

AN

AMERICAN SLAVE.

WRITTEN BY HIMSELF.

BOSTON:
PUBLISHED AT THE ANTI-SLAVERY OFFICE,
NO. 25 CORNHILL
1845.

Frederick's first autobiography was published
in 1845 when he was 27 years old

Yet, he missed his family, and he wanted to work for the abolition of American slavery while in America. When he decided to return home, his British friends were alarmed—surely he would be captured when he reached the United States. Two women, sisters-in-law Ellen and Mrs. Henry Richardson organized the fundraising that not only provided money to purchase Douglass's freedom, but also enough to allow him to purchase a printing press.

Chapter Seven
A Free Man and Editor Reads the U.S. Constitution

Douglass had spent nearly two years in the British Isles. In 1847, as he left Liverpool, England, for America, he was no longer a fugitive slave, but a free man. The funds collected by his English friends had secured his freedom. It cost one hundred and fifty pounds sterling (approximately $19,500 in 2016). Before sailing home, he had his manumission papers signed by Thomas and Hugh Auld.

Letters from strict abolitionists were published in the British and American press criticizing Douglass for his compensated emancipation. Douglass answered by pointing out that he was paying his kidnappers and captors a ransom, rather than believing that human beings could be bought and sold.

Even as a free man, Douglass experienced racism on his return trip on the steamer Cambria, where he was forced to stay in steerage again even though he had paid for a first class cabin. The Cunard line that owned the Cambria was criticized in editorials throughout the United Kingdom for it. Mr. Samuel Cunard, owner of the shipping line, wrote Douglass a letter of apology for the behavior of his employees.

Douglass had expressed to Garrison his intention to launch his own antislavery newspaper. His former mentor discouraged him and his

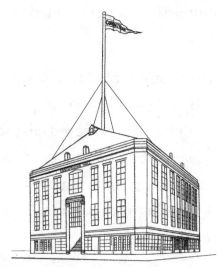

Hundreds of people packed Corinthian Hall in Rochester to hear Frederick speak

friends told him that he was better suited to oratory, and that any newspaper effort was doomed to failure. But Douglass was determined; he left New England and moved to Rochester, New York, to start his new paper.

Douglass chose the name *North Star* for the only guide fugitive slaves had on their journey to freedom. Its first issue appeared on December 3, 1847. In it, Douglass wrote about the character of the United States Constitution and how voting could make change happen. By 1851, after much study and debate, Douglass decided that the words of the Constitution made slavery unconstitutional.

On July 5, 1852, Douglass gave one of the most famous and important speeches of his life. The title was "What to the Slave is the Fourth of July?" Between five hundred and six hundred people attended the lecture in Rochester, New York's Corinthian Hall. Tickets cost 12 1/2 cents per person, which amounted to $3.68 in 2016.

In the lecture, Douglass told the story of Independence Day from "the slave's point of view."

It showed the irony in celebrating American independence while the nation held millions of people in bondage.

Chapter Eight
Douglass's Public and Private Lives

Even though Douglass wrote three autobiographies, he concentrated on his public experiences rather than his private ones. His life stories reveal little of the family he created with his wife, Anna Murray Douglass. His work for the Massachusetts Anti-Slavery Society kept Douglass away from home for long periods of time, and Anna was left to raise their children alone. Frederick wrote to her regularly, and he sent her money for expenses.

Anna took good care of her children and of the household in New Bedford, where their first three children were born. Rosetta Douglass was born in 1839,

Rosetta Douglas, Frederick's oldest daughter, would read and write for her mother

Lewis Henry Douglass in 1840, and Frederick Douglass, Jr., in 1842. By the time their third son was born in 1844, the Douglass family had moved to Lynn, Massachusetts. This son was named Charles Remond Douglass.

The youngest Douglass child, Annie, was born in 1849, after the family established a new home in Rochester, New York. Annie, perhaps Douglass's favorite child, died at the age of eleven while her father was in England for a second time. He received this devastating news by post and returned home immediately.

Anna Douglass had never learned to read, although Frederick had tried to teach her. It became Rosetta's job to read her father's letters to her mother and to write down Anna's reply to her husband's letters. Rosetta would later put her early skills to good use by becoming a schoolteacher.

When he was at home in Rochester, Douglass worked at his paper, the *North Star*. At its most successful, the *North Star* circulated about 4,000 copies. Threatened with financial ruin, Douglass mortgaged his house to keep it going. Generous sponsors donated money as well, but the person who helped the most was Mrs. Julia Griffiths Crofts. Douglass's English friend was an abolitionist who traveled to America to help Douglass run the paper. Her management helped pull it out of its financial problems.

Charles Douglass was Frederick's youngest son

In addition to writing, publishing, editing, and lecturing, Douglass acted as a stationmaster and conductor on the Underground Railroad.

The Underground Railroad was a series of safe houses where fugitive slaves could find food, shelter, and support on their way to freedom. At one time, Douglass and Anna harbored as many as eleven fugitives in their Rochester home.

Even though Rochester was one of the better places in the United States for African Americans to live, there was still racial prejudice in their day-to-day lives. Douglass's children's education posed problems for him. He managed to have Rosetta admitted to a prestigious Christian school for girls, the Tracy Seminary. But Douglass was outraged to learn that Rosetta was confined to a room alone.

He confronted the schoolmistress, Miss Tracy, about his daughter's mistreatment. Although only one set of parents objected to including Rosetta with the rest of the girls, she was no longer allowed to attend the Tracy Seminary.

Douglass also had trouble placing his children in the public school located in the district where he lived, owned property, and paid taxes. They could only attend an inferior public school for

African American children—one far from their home. This was an unacceptable situation, and Douglass fought against it with speeches and editorials in his paper.

Frederick Douglass Jr., Frederick's middle son, became Frederick's namesake

In the meantime, his children were educated privately at his own expense. Finally he obtained a hearing before the Board of Education, and after much effort, he won his cause: black children and white children were able to attend public school together in their home districts in the city of Rochester.

Douglass accomplished other goals for free African Americans in the city of Rochester. He worked for equal admission to public entertainments like museums, parks, and public lectures from which blacks had been excluded. All in all, he was happy with the gains he had made on the local level in Rochester, for the sake of his own children as well as all the people of the city.

Frederick never stopped speaking against slavery and advocating for the rights of all Americans

Chapter Nine
My Bondage and My Freedom and the 1850s

Douglass's second autobiography, _My Bondage and My Freedom_, was published in 1855, ten years after he had published his first autobiography. He was a very different Douglass than the young fugitive slave who wrote the _Narrative_. He had gained a reputation as a leader of the Northern

James McCune Smith was Frederick's colleague at the Anti-Slavery Society and helped him build a name for himself

free black and civil rights reform communities. He had earned this reputation in part by being a member of the American Anti-Slavery Society alongside his colleague James McCune Smith.

So, why did Douglass feel that it was necessary to write a second autobiography? One reason might have been that he became much more involved in the public discussion of slavery, especially the status of slavery in the expanding western territories of the United States (areas like Kansas had not yet become states).

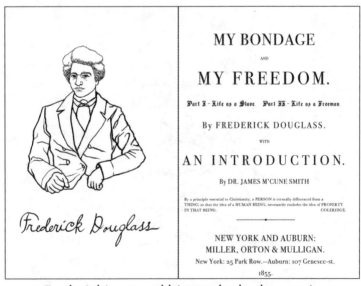

Frederick's second biography had a part in influencing slavery policies in the new territories

He voiced his opinions on hotly debated issues like the Compromise of 1850, which decided the fate (slave or free) of the territories gained by the United States in the Mexican War (1846–48). He also weighed in on the Kansas-Nebraska Act of 1854, the Act that repealed the Missouri Compromise of 1820.

The book motivated even more people to question Douglass about what it had been like to be a slave. As they had with the first autobiography, family members of his former masters in Maryland claimed his descriptions of slavery were untrue.

Though *My Bondage and My Freedom* did not sell as many copies as Douglass's *Narrative*, it was very popular with American reviewers and readers. Some compared it to the best-selling novel, Harriet Beecher Stowe's *Uncle Tom's Cabin*.

In the years following the publication of *My Bondage and My Freedom*, tensions increased over slavery. In 1857, the Supreme Court decision in the infamous Dred Scott v. Sandford case, ruled that, according to the Constitution, African

Americans had no rights that the federal government was obligated to uphold. This decision horrified abolitionists.

Harriet Beecher Stowe wrote *Uncle Tom's Cabin,* a fiction book denouncing slavery

In 1859, Douglass's friend John Brown attempted to launch a widespread violent and armed slave rebellion by seizing a U.S. arsenal and its ammunition at Harpers Ferry, Virginia. He and his men were defeated by federal troops led by Colonel Robert E. Lee. Brown had stayed at Douglass's home and tried unsuccessfully to win Douglass's support.

John Brown wanted to launch a violent slave
rebellion to force freedom into the South

Douglass fled to Canada and boarded a
steamer to England in order to escape certain ar-
rest for his known association with Brown, even
though he was in Philadelphia during the raid on
Harpers Ferry. But Douglass's stay in England
was brief: soon he received the terrible news that
his youngest child, Annie, had died. Douglass returned to America to mourn his daughter and in
time to witness the 1860 presidential election.

Chapter Ten
The Election of 1860, the Civil War, and African American Soldiers

Slavery was a major issue in the Presidential election of 1860. Even though Abraham Lincoln's Republican platform fell far short of endorsing emancipation, he, unlike the other two candidates, did not support slavery's growth and geographical spread. This position gave Douglass reason to hope.

Following Lincoln's election in November of 1860, South Carolina seceded, or left, the Union in December of 1860. By February 1861, Mississippi, Florida, Alabama, Georgia, Louisiana, and Texas had joined South Carolina, forming the Confederate States of America with Jefferson Davis as their elected Confederate President. When Lincoln was inaugurated as President of the United States on March 4, 1861, he faced a serious rival and certain war.

War came on April 12, 1861, when the Confederate Army opened fire on Fort Sumter, a federal garrison on Charleston Bay in South Carolina. The American Civil War had begun, and it would last until May 10, 1865. Although Frederick Douglass would not fight in the war, he played an important role in the Union victory and the abolition of slavery.

The Civil War officially began when the Confederate Army attacked Fort Sumter

Douglass knew that a key to a Northern victory was to admit African American men to the army and to train them to fight for their freedom. Douglass wrote many editorials urging the government to declare the war an abolition war and to make use of the strength and courage of American blacks, free and slave.

Lewis Douglass, Frederick's oldest son, joined the Union army in the African American regiments

Eventually, Lincoln granted Governor Andrew of Massachusetts permission to form two regiments of African American soldiers, the 54th and 55th. Douglass's sons, Charles and Lewis, were among the first two African American men to enlist in the new regiments.

Still, dire problems remained and Douglass wrote letters to his powerful acquaintances demanding equality for soldiers of color. As a result, Douglass was invited to the White House to

Douglass convinced President Lincoln to form two
African American regiments to allow former slaves
to fight for their own freedom

discuss the grievances of black soldiers in person.
On August 10, 1863 Douglass met Abraham Lin-
coln for the first time. To his surprise, a nervous
Douglass found the President easy to approach.

When he first saw Lincoln, he looked over-
worked and tired, but his face lit up with the
mention of Douglass's name. The President rose
from his chair and extended his hand in wel-
come. At that moment, Douglass wrote, he felt
himself "in the presence of an honest man"—a
man he could trust without doubt.

Douglass told the President that it was becoming harder and harder to get men of color to enlist. They did not receive the same promotions or wages that white soldiers received. The government did not retaliate upon Confederate soldiers when black soldiers were captured, shot, or hung.

Lincoln listened silently and patiently to Douglass's words, and he replied carefully and thoughtfully to each of the particulars of Douglass's grievances, explaining white prejudices, the fear of increasing Confederate retaliation, and promising promotions upon the Secretary of War's recommendation. Though Douglass did not agree with all of the President's decisions, he decided that he could still go on recruiting men of color in good conscience.

When Lincoln was reelected to the Presidency for a second term, Douglass, against the warnings of several friends, attended the festivities of the second inaugural. Seeing Douglass enter, Lincoln announced to all around him, "Here comes my friend Douglass." The President took

Douglass had great respect for
President Abraham Lincoln

him by the hand and asked him his opinion of
the Inaugural Speech.

Douglass heard the terrible news of President
Lincoln's assassination in April of 1865, while
in Rochester, New York. At the City Hall, surrounded by Rochester's leading citizens, Douglass shared the podium with well-known white
orators to express the country's grief and offer

prayers. He was amazed at the power of the tragedy to make both white and black speakers feel like members of one family.

The Thirteenth Amendment to the U.S. Constitution was passed by Congress on January 31, 1865 and ratified by the states on December 6, 1865. It abolished slavery. The formal end of the Civil War was declared by President Andrew Johnson on August 20, 1866. Much had changed in Douglass's lifetime.

He began to receive many invitations to speak at colleges, lecture halls, and literary societies. Unlike his speeches for the American Anti-Slavery Society, for which he was paid very little, these opportunities offered as much as two hundred dollars per speech. One speech Douglass delivered was a particular favorite among audiences: "The Trials and Triumphs of Self-Made Men." He delivered this speech with small changes for more than thirty-five years during his long speaking career.

The speech encouraged people to work hard and to grasp all opportunities for education and elevation that came their way. Douglass drew on his own experiences as well as those of other men, black and white, who had been born into degraded situations and who had used their labor and ingenuity to raise themselves by means of their own constant efforts.

Vice President Andrew Johnson took over as president after Lincoln's assassination

Overall though, Douglass believed that African Americans would not truly be free until they had full access to the "Ballot-box, the Jury-box, and the Cartridge-box." In other words, African Americans needed to exercise citizenship by voting, serving on juries during trials, and having the right to bear arms to protect their lives and property. Douglass considered the right to vote of the utmost importance, and he set to work to secure it.

This was his agenda on February 7th, 1866, when he visited the White House to interview President Andrew Johnson on the topic. Hopes were high, but Frederick was disappointed when Johnson gave a prepared speech without answering any questions.

Douglass's second step in pursuit of voting rights was his attendance as a delegate to the National Loyalists' Convention in Philadelphia in September 1866. His election by the City of Rochester to represent them at a national political convention was a shock to Douglass and the rest of the country. He was the first African American delegate.

When Douglass was called upon to speak, he told the convention that giving American blacks the vote would be the only way to prevent them from a return to slavery. The issue became part of the Republican Party policy and in 1868, when former Union General Ulysses S. Grant was elected President of the United States, the issue of African American male voting (suffrage) was recommended as the Fifteenth Amendment to the United States Constitution.

President Ulysses S. Grant had been a Union general in the Civil War and helped ratify the Fifteenth Amendment guaranteeing all men the right to vote

The Amendment was ratified on February 3rd, 1870. By law, African American men were entitled to all of the benefits of American citizenship. Unfortunately, however, many were unable to practice those rights because of violent opposition.

Chapter Eleven
A Turbulent Decade,
1870 Through 1880

After the passage of the Fifteenth Amendment to the U.S. Constitution, many of Douglass's friends urged him to move to the South, where there was a large African American population who could now vote him into office. Douglass ultimately decided against moving to the South partially because of his age, but also to avoid being called a carpet-bagger, or opportunist. Douglass valued deeply the respect he had spent his entire public life working to gain. He did not want to sacrifice it.

Instead, Douglass decided to become editor-in-chief of the *New National Era,* a weekly newspaper in Washington, D.C. The newspaper was dedicated to informing and educating American blacks who had recently become voters. Douglass was proud of the contents of the newspaper and of its many accomplished African American contributors. The first issue appeared on January 13, 1870 and it lasted successfully for four years. It went out of business permanently on October 22, 1874. This was Douglass' last try at publishing a newspaper.

The year 1874 witnessed yet another failure for Frederick Douglass. Congress had established a bank called the Freedman's Savings and Trust

Frederick dedicated the Freedmen's Memorial to President Lincoln in a ceremony in 1876

Company, which eventually opened thirty-seven branches in seventeen states to serve former slaves. However, in 1873, bank corruption was discovered.

Freedman's Bank was opened in 1865 to serve former slaves, but closed in 1874 due to corruption

To restore public confidence, Douglass was appointed as bank president, but despite his efforts, the bank failed in July 1874. Along with the other investors, Frederick lost a great deal of money. Though blameless, Douglass had to endure the humiliation of discussing his involvement with the bank before Senate investigation hearings in 1880.

Still, the honors balanced the defeats. He was appointed a delegate on a mission to the Dominican Republic, then called Santo Domingo, to determine whether it should be annexed to the US. Although it was not annexed, President Grant

President Rutherford B. Hayes appointed Frederick the Marshal of the District of Columbia

and Frederick both favored the annexation, which would spread American democracy.

Additional honors of the 1870s were Douglass's appointment as member of the Council for the Government of the District of Columbia; his election as elector at large for New York; speaking at the monument of the unknown loyal dead at Arlington; and his address at the unveiling of the Lincoln Monument.

Douglass was appointed to the post of United States Marshal of the District of Columbia by President Rutherford B. Hayes who had been declared the winner in the presidential election in 1876. In June of 1877, Marshal Frederick Douglass returned after more than forty years to St. Michaels in Talbot County, Maryland. When he arrived, he received a message that his elderly former master, Thomas Auld, desired to meet with him. Douglass agreed and he had long desired a reunion with Auld.

Douglass wrote, "...I regarded him as I did myself, a victim of the circumstances of birth, education, law, and custom." Douglass forgave Auld, realizing that even slaveholders had no control over the times and situations into which they had been born.

Douglass was led to Auld's bedroom, where the two men shook hands and addressed each other formally, as "Captain Auld" and "Marshal Douglass." Both men were deeply moved — Auld even wept. When asked, he thought Frederick had been born sometime in February of 1818. If Auld's memory was correct, Douglass was one

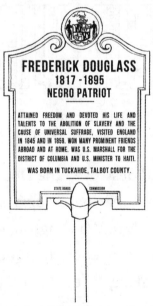

Talbot County, Maryland, has a sign highlighting the history of Frederick Douglass's life, but it has the wrong birth year

year younger than he had always believed himself to be. He would never know that Auld had been right.

Frederick Douglass' house "Cedar Hill" in Anacostia outside of Washington D.C.

After fire had destroyed the Douglass's house in Rochester in 1872 the Douglass family relocated permanently to Washington, D.C. By 1878, Douglass was earning enough money to relax his demanding speaking schedule and to buy a new home. He bought a white frame house in the vil-

In the back of Cedar Hill was a small cabin
named the Growlery House where
Frederick went to read and write

lage of Uniontown near the Anacostia River and
named the new residence Cedar Hill.

Douglass was hopeful that he could remain
in the prestigious position of U.S. Marshal after James A. Garfield won the 1880 presidential
election. But it was not to be—Garfield removed
Douglass from the marshal's office and appointed
him to the less impressive post of Recorder of
Deeds for the District of Columbia.

When President James Garfield became president,
he appointed Frederick the Recorder of Deeds

In June of 1881, Douglass visited the Eastern
Shore yet again. This time he went to Wye House,
the Great House on the Lloyd plantation where
he had first been introduced to the hardships of
slavery. He recalled early memories which made
their way into his final autobiography, *Life and
Times of Frederick Douglass,* published in 1881.

When Frederick Douglass saw the first edition of his third autobiography, he was angry. The
quality of the paper and the binding was shoddy.
He was even more upset over the illustrations
that appeared in the book. Douglass, always so

careful in his self-presentation, found them insulting and degrading. Relatively low sales were a discouraging sign that many Americans had grown weary of discussing racial injustices, slavery, and the Civil War.

Frederick argued for the Civil Rights Act of 1875 in Lincoln Hall in front of more than 2,000 people

Near the end of 1883 the judicial branch of the federal government reflected clearly the decreasing national interest in human rights. In October, the United States Supreme Court declared the Civil Rights Act of 1875 unconstitutional. It had been passed to guarantee the enforcement of the Fourteenth Amendment, granting the benefits of citizenship to all African Americans. The law stated that all citizens, regardless of race or color, were entitled to equal access to all public facilities such as places of lodging, of amusement, and modes of transportation.

Douglass was outraged by the decision and spoke out against it in one of the largest meetings on the subject, at Lincoln Hall in Washington, D.C. on October 22, 1883. Over 2,000 people of all races attended the meeting. Another 2,000 were turned away due to lack of space in the auditorium. When speaking, Douglass emphasized the feelings of betrayal that he and seventy million people felt.

Chapter Twelve
<u>Final Years</u>

In early July of 1882, Anna Murray Douglass suffered a stroke, which paralyzed the entire left side of her body. She died less than a month after the attack, on August 4, 1882. She was sixty-nine years old. After her funeral in Washington, Douglass, along with their children and grandchildren, accompanied her casket on the train to their former home of Rochester, New York, where her burial took place.

After his first wife died, Frederick controversially married Helen Pitts, a white woman

During and after the Civil War, American women had begun to work outside the home. In 1882, Douglass had hired a new clerk to work in the Office of the Recorder of Deeds. Her name was Helen Pitts, a graduate of Mount Holyoke Seminary, a former teacher, and the daughter of white abolitionists. Her uncle, Hiram Pitts, was Douglass's next-door neighbor. Douglass and Helen supported many causes in common—women's rights, race equality, and temperance.

His friendship with Helen grew deeper and stronger during their two years of work together, and they decided to marry. Because interracial marriage was so controversial at the time, the couple decided to wed privately, without fanfare, by Reverend Francis Grimké. On January 24, 1884, they were married at the parsonage of the Fifteenth Street Presbyterian

Reverend
Francis Grimké

Church, the most prestigious African American church in the nation.

When widely criticized, Douglass spoke out—he asked why he should be criticized for marrying a woman of his father's race rather than his mother's. Worse, neither the Douglass children nor the Pitts family supported the marriage. Helen's Uncle Hiram disowned her, and Douglass's children coldly avoided their father's new wife as much as possible.

In September of 1886 Douglass and Helen embarked on an overseas tour, which would take them first through Europe and then to Egypt, a country with which Douglass had long been fascinated. On the trip he reported seeing many similarities of people of varied races and ethnicities the world over. He concluded that human beings have more traits in common than they have differences.

The Douglasses returned to the United States in 1887, in time for the presidential campaign of 1888. Douglass traveled and spoke on behalf of the Republican Party, the traditional champion of antislavery and civil rights legislation. His support and the support of other black leaders helped Republican candidate Benjamin Harrison, grandson of President William Henry Harrison, become the twenty-third president of the United States.

In 1889, President Harrison appointed Douglass to the office of Minister Resident and Consul General to the Republic of Haiti. The US wanted a naval base there. Later Douglass wrote that that post and his appointment by Haitian

President Benjamin Harrison appointed Frederick to yet another new job, Minister Resident and Consul General to the Republic of Haiti

President Hippolyte to represent Haiti at the World's Columbian Exposition were his "crowning honors."

Haiti's President Florvil Hippolyte further honored Frederick by appointing him to represent Haiti at the World's Columbian Exposition

In Douglass's address at the exposition, he told the story of Haiti's rise from a slave colony to a free country of its own. He encouraged the United States to support Haiti and follow it to freedom. As in many of his speeches, he told the story of the slave, the story of nineteenth-century America. Abolitionists, slaveholders, racism, law, and war were common in his speeches.

He always spoke about the human rights of all Americans: men and women, blacks and whites, immigrants and native-born. Douglass's speeches told the story of progress, not only of his own race's rise from slavery, but the whole country's. He discussed how conditions for free blacks worsened in the Southern states and how a mass migration to the North was not the answer.

Toward the end of his life, inspired by a friendship with activist Ida B. Wells, Douglass spoke out fervently against the crime of lynching. One of his final speeches, "Lessons of the Hour," delivered a year before his death, lamented the loss of civil rights in the South, since the Democratic Party, the old slave-holding party, had regained strength. He spoke now to crowds of the fact that peace brought a new type of slavery— fear of widespread racist violence in the South.

Ida B. Wells

On February 20, 1895, Douglass attended a women's rights rally in Washington, D.C. There, Susan B. Anthony, a leader in women's suffrage, escorted her old friend to the platform. He returned to Cedar Hill to dine with Helen, and the couple waited for a carriage to take them to a meeting at a neighborhood church. As Douglass practiced his speech for the evening, he crumpled to the floor. He had suffered a sudden attack—either a heart attack or stroke—and he had died instantly.

News of Douglass's death spread quickly, and telegrams and letters of condolence from both famous people and ordinary citizens flooded the lovely home he had shared with Helen. Four days later, the schools in Washington, D.C. were closed for the funeral of one of the most influential Americans of the nineteenth century. His body lay in an open casket in the Metropolitan African Methodist Episcopal Church, and thousands of people, including many school children, filed past the great man to pay their respects.

Frederick spent many hours in his personal library
preparing speeches or reading

That evening, Douglass's children and Helen accompanied his body on a train to Rochester, where he was to be buried. In Rochester, the body lay in state in City Hall and a second funeral was held in the Central Church. Douglass was buried in Mount Hope Cemetery in Rochester, near the graves of his first wife Anna and his daughter, Annie. His grave stone bore the mark of slavery—his date of birth had never been corrected, and its inscription read, "To the memory of Frederick Douglass, 1817–1895."

After her husband's death, Helen worked to preserve Douglass's belongings and writings at the Cedar Hill House in Anacostia, Washington, D.C. The house is now a part of the National Parks Service, functioning as a museum and archive of Douglass's life's work.

TO THE MEMORY OF
FREDERICK DOUGLASS
1817 — 1895
ERECTED BY HIS SONS
LEWIS H & CHARLES R

DOUGLASS

Frederick was buried with his first wife, Anna, in Mount Hope Cemetery in Rochester, New York

Select Quotes from Frederick Douglass

"What, to the American slave is your 4th of July? I answer: a day that reveals to him, more than all other days in the year, the gross injustice and cruelty to which he is the constant victim. To him, your celebration is a sham;...a thin veil to cover up crimes that would disgrace a nation of savages. There is not a nation on the earth guilty of practices, more shocking and bloody, than are the people of these United States, at this very hour." – *From his speech* "What to the Slave is the Fourth of July?" *on July 5, 1852*

"If there is no struggle, there is no progress. Those who profess to favor freedom and yet depreciate agitation, are men who want crops without plowing up the ground, they want rain without thunder and lightning. They want the ocean without the roar of its many waters." – *From his speech* "West India Emancipation" *on August 3, 1857*

"[A] woman should have every honorable motive to exertion which is enjoyed by man, to the full extent of her capacities and endowments. The case is too plain for argument. Nature has given woman the same powers...." – *From the* "Frederick Douglass' Paper", *on June 10, 1853*

"Any man can be brave when there is no danger." – *From* "In The Words of Frederick Douglass"

"Right is of no sex—Truth is of no color—God is the Father of us all, and we are all Brethren." – *The slogan of the* "North Star"

Frederick Douglass Timeline

1818 Frederick Augustus Washington Bailey born at Holme Hill Farm

1824 Sent to live on Lloyd Plantation, Wye River, at the home of his master, Aaron Anthony

1826 Sent to live with Hugh Auld family in Fells Point section of Baltimore

1827 Anthony's slaves divided among his heirs; Frederick awarded to Thomas Auld; returned to Baltimore

1827 Sophia Auld teaches Frederick his letters; later he learns to write and do arithmetic on his own

1835 Hired out to work for William Freeland, a Talbot County, Maryland, farmer. Secretly organizes Sabbath school and teaches other slaves to read.

1836 Escape plot fails; Frederick jailed in Easton, Maryland

1836 Sent back to Baltimore by Thomas Auld

1838 Escapes to the North by train and boat, marries Anna Murray in New York City, and moves to New Bedford, Massachusetts

1838 Changes name to Frederick Douglass

1842 Hired as antislavery lecturer after 3,500 mile tour draws big crowds/support

1845 *Narrative of the Life of Frederick Douglass, an American Slave* published

1845 Travels to England, to avoid capture or return to slavery & spreads antislavery cause in British Isles.

1846 Becomes free man when manumission papers are filed in Baltimore County court

World Timeline

1817   New York Stock Exchange is founded

1824   Britain and the US attempt to agree on a treaty to suppress slavery

1826   The world's first photograph is taken

1827   New York passes a law to emancipate slaves

1835   Spain and Britain unite against the slave trade

1836   Republic of Texas officially abolishes slavery, but people still practiced slavery

1838   Cherokee Indians walk the "Trail of Tears" 1,000 miles from Tennessee to Oklahoma

1839   English scientist John William Draper takes the first photograph of the moon

1840   The US reports it has over 1,200 cotton factories

1842   The volcano, Mt. St. Helens, erupts in Washington

1842   The University of Notre Dame is founded in Indiana

1844   The telegraph is patented

1845   The potato famine in Ireland begins

1845   Florida and Texas become the 27th and 28th states of the United States

1845   Baseball defines its first set of rules

Frederick Douglass Timeline (cont.)

1855   Publishes second of his autobiographies, *My Bondage and My Freedom*

1860   Returns to United States upon learning of March 13th death of 11-year-old daughter Annie

1861   The Civil War begins, Douglass begins agitating for African Americans to be eligible for military service for the Union.

1863   Becomes an agent for the U.S. Government to recruit African American soldiers into the Union Army. He visits President Lincoln in White House

1865   Speaks at Memorial Meeting on Life and Death of Lincoln after denied African Americans participation in Lincoln funeral procession through New York

1865   Douglass Institute, a Baltimore school for Negro children is established in his honor

1874   Named President of Freedman's Bank

1877   Appointment by President Hayes as US Marshal for D.C.

1881   Publishes 3rd autobiography: *Life and Times of Frederick Douglass*

1881   Appointed by President Garfield to be Recorder of Deeds for D.C.

1884   Marries Helen Pitts, his white former secretary

1894   Delivers his last great address, "Lessons of the Hour," against lynch law in the South

1895   Dies suddenly

World Timeline (cont.)

1860   Abraham Lincoln elected president

1861   US Civil War begins

1863   The Emancipation Proclamation frees slaves in Confederate states

1865   US Civil War ends. Abraham Lincoln is assassinated

1865   The US Secret Service is created

1871   Yellowstone National Park, the first national park is created

1877   The last of the Union troops are withdrawn from former Confederate states

1881   US President James A. Garfield is shot and later dies from complications

1882   The 1st Labor Day parade happens

1892   Ida B. Wells, journalist investigates lynchings in Tennessee

1895   W.E.B. Du Bois becomes the first African American to receive a Ph.D. from Harvard University

Glossary

Abolition   Movement urging and working to end slavery; the act of abolishing or doing away with; advocates were called abolitionists

Assassination   Deliberate and public murder of a prominent and usually political figure

Civil War   A war from 1861 to 1865 in the United States between the Northern and Southern states about whether new states should be allowed to have slaves or not

Columbian Orator, The   19th-century children's textbook with samples of classical and English speeches that were memorized and recited by students

Compromise of 1850   Five separate bills which decided free or slave state status for California, Utah, what is now New Mexico, and the Texas Panhandle (US territories acquired in the Mexican-American War, 1846-1848)

Confederacy   South Carolina, Mississippi, Florida, Alabama, Georgia, Louisiana, and Texas (signed The Confederate Constitution March 11, 1861) seceding from the United States to form their own government – after the Battle of Fort Sumter – joined by Virginia, Arkansas, Tennessee, and North Carolina.

Constitution   Document with fundamental principles that govern a country

Dred Scott v. Sandford Case   United States Supreme Court landmark case ruling (1857) that no one of African descent could have the rights that whites would recognize, and as such had no right sue in a federal court

Emancipation   Legal freeing of slaves; applied to specific states. After the Civil War, the 13th Amendment made this a national law

Fugitives   Escaped slaves; 1793 and 1850 laws covered their freedom and rights to free status

Inaugural   Marking the beginning, as in an inaugural speech

Inauguration   Ceremony dedicating someone to office, usually with an oath and fanfare

Kansas-Nebraska Act of 1854   Repealed, or reversed the Missouri Compromise of 1820; allowed Nebraska and Kansas to decide by popular sovereignty whether they would be slave or free states

Lecture   A formal speech on a topic of interest; popular 19th-century event

Liberator, The   William Lloyd Garrison's weekly newspaper (1831-1865) dedicated to abolition and complete emancipation of slaves. Seventy-five percent of 3,000 circulation was from African American subscribers

Manumission Papers   Formal papers releasing a slave who had purchased his freedom; papers stating an African American was no longer a slave, but a free person

Missouri Compromise   Federal decision to allow slavery in new state Missouri and deny it in the other land (which became Southwest states) acquired in the Louisiana Land Purchase; Passed as a law in 1820 and repealed in 1850 by the Kansas Nebraska Act

Oration   A speech generally intended to inspire, motivate, and/or educate on a weighty topic; orators delivered these speeches

Plantation   A large farm where crops were grown, and often tended by slaves for landowner profit

Supreme Court of the United States   Federally appointed judges whose rulings stand as the highest or final legal decisions

Territories of the United States   Acquired land that had not yet been granted statehood

Uncle Tom's Cabin   1851 abolitionist novel by Harriet Beecher Stowe; sold 300,000 copies US and 1 million in Britain in 1851; false claims were made that it "started the Civil War"

Underground Railroad   Network of abolitionists that arranged escape, shelter, and aid to slaves running away and seeking freedom

Union   The states that did not secede from the United States; also the entire United States

Bibliography

Douglass, Frederick. *Autobiographical Writings*. The Frederick Douglass Papers, 2nd ser., edited by John W. Blassingame, Peter P. Hinks, and John R. McKivigan. 3 vols. New Haven: Yale University Press, 1999-2012.

McFeely, William S. *Frederick Douglass*. New York: W.W. Norton, 1991.

Preston, Dickson J. *Young Frederick Douglass: The Maryland Years*. Baltimore: Johns Hopkins University Press, 1985.

Further Reading

Davis, Ossie. *Escape to Freedom: A Play about Young Frederick Douglass*. New York: Puffin Books, 1990.

Muller, John. *Frederick Douglass in Washington, D.C.: The Lion of Anacostia*. Mount Pleasant, South Carolina: The History Press, 2012.

National Geographic Learning. *Voice of Freedom: A Story About Frederick Douglass*. Springfield, Missouri: 21st Century, 2001.

Russell, Sharman Apt. *Frederick Douglass. Black Americans of Achievement*. New York: Chelsea House Publications, 1988.

Index

A

Abolition, abolitionists, 18–19
African American soldiers, 74–77
Allender's Jake, 43
American Anti-Slavery Society, 68
Andersen, Hans Christian, 54
Anthony, Susan B., 101
Anthony family, 4–5, 7, 12
Auld family, 7, 9–16, 22–24, 24–25, 33, 35–37, 38–39, 57, 88–89
Autobiographies, vii–viii, 53, 55, 67–69, 92–93

B

Brown, John, 70–71

C

Civil rights, viii, 64–66, 80–82, 93–94
Civil War, 74, 79
Collins, John A., 51
The Columbian Orator, 17–18
Confederate States of America, 73
Constitution, U.S., 59
Covey, Edward, 26–28
Crofts, Julia Griffiths, 63

D

Davis, Jefferson, 73
Douglass, Frederick, as free man. See also Family, of Douglass
    abolitionist career, 67–69
    civil rights career, viii, 64–66, 80–82, 93–94
    death of, 101–102
    in Europe, 54–56, 71, 97
    freedom purchased, 56–57
    government career, vii, viii, 87–88, 91, 97–99
    influence of, ix–x
    lecture career, vii, 51–52, 54–55, 59–60, 79–80, 99–101
    and Lincoln, 75–78
    name change, 45–46
    in New Bedford, 47–48
    in New York, 42–44